Body Language

Master Body Language

A Practical Guide to Understanding Nonverbal Communication and Improving Your Relationships

Antony Felix

Your Free Gift

As a way of thanking you for the purchase, I'd like to offer you a complimentary gift:

- **5 Pillar Life Transformation Checklist:** This short book is about life transformation, presented in bit size pieces for easy implementation. I believe that without such a checklist, you are likely to have a hard time implementing anything in this book and any other thing you set out to do religiously and sticking to it for the long haul. It doesn't matter whether your goals relate to weight loss, relationships, personal finance, investing, personal development, improving communication in your family, your overall health, finances, improving your sex life, resolving issues in your relationship, fighting PMS successfully, investing, running a successful business, traveling etc. With a checklist like this one, you can bet that anything you do will seem a lot easier to implement until the end. Therefore, even if you don't continue reading this book, at least read the one thing that will help you in every other aspect of your life. Grab your copy now by clicking/tapping here or simply enter http://bit.ly/2fantonfreebie into your browser. Your life will never be the same again (if you implement what's in this book), I promise.

PS: I'd like your feedback. If you are happy with this book, please leave a review on Amazon.

Introduction

This book contains proven steps and strategies on how to understand nonverbal communication and improve your relationships.

Actions, they say, speak louder than words.

Communication has two major categories: verbal and non-verbal communication. **While most people fully understand the concept of verbal communication, many are yet to grasp the concept and importance of non-verbal communication through body language communication.**

Before I became aware of my body language and how I used it, or rather, misused it to communicate, I thought I was *"The most misunderstood person in the world"* because somehow, people always managed to misinterpret and twist my words to mean something different than what I intended. More often than not, their misinterpreted implications gravitated towards the negative.

Before I achieved the self-awareness that comes from being adept at using body language, I could be saying something very nice but my 'attitude' and physical disposition made it look like I was being rude, condescending, or even sarcastic.

Until I dissected my habitual negative use of my body language, I found it very difficult to keep and

maintain friendships. That was a while back and since then, I have taken it upon myself to learn and grasp the concept of non-verbal communication especially body language communication and how it can make or break relationships.

This book contains all the body language secrets I have learned through my many years of consistent body language practice. *The book details how I transformed myself into a powerful speaker and built a strong network simply by improving my body language skills. It details how you can use the same proven and tested strategies to improve your nonverbal communication and improve your work and personal relationships.*

More precisely, in this book, you will learn:

- Why you need to prioritize your mastery of your body language

- The different parts of your body that greatly contribute to communication

- The elements of body language communication

- Gender disparity in body language communication

- How to 'read' people like open books in business and professional settings

- How to master your body language in business

- How to 'read' people like open books in social and personal relationship settings

- How to master your body language in personal relationships

- Mistakes to avoid

- And much, much more!

If you are passionate about being able to read people's innermost desires and thought patterns without them even realizing it then using that to optimize your body language, this book is for you!

Let's begin!

I hope you enjoy it!

Table of Contents

Your Free Gift — 2

Introduction — 3

Body Language For Beginners — 10

What Is Body Language? — 13

    Importance of Body Language — 13

How Different Parts of Your Body Contribute to Communication — 16

Elements of Body Language Communication — 16

    Facial Body Language — 16

    Facial Body Language — 17

    Eye Expression — 28

    Gestures — 34

    Body Posture — 43

    Voice — 46

    Appearance — 46

    Touch — 47

The Art Of Smiling — 48

    The Magic Of Smiling _____ 50

The Power Of Your Hands _____ 56

    How Handshakes And Palms Contribute To Your General Body Language _____ 56

Rules For Accurate Reading Of Body Language _____ 61

Gender Disparity in Body Language Communication _____ 64

    Facial Expressions _____ 64

    Proximity _____ 64

    Male Body Language _____ 65

    Female Body Language _____ 68

The Most Common Female And Male Courtship Gestures And Signals _____ 72

    Common Female Courtship Gestures And Signals _____ 72

Common Male Courtship Gestures And Signals _____ 81

Body Language In Business: How To Use Body Language To Achieve Business Success _____ 86

- Eye Contact and Listening Techniques 86
- Mirroring 87
- Palms Facing Down 87
- Wide Stance 88
- Smiling 88
- Body Movements 89
- Handshakes 89

Handshake Styles To Communicate Control And Dominance 90

The Intimacy And Control Handshakes 97

Cultural Gesture Differences 103

The Most Common Cross-Cultural Gestures 104

The Language Of Hands 107

Body Language And Love: How To Use Body Language To Nurture Personal Relationships 113

- Positive 'Love' Body Language: Men 113
- Negative 'Love' Body Language: Men 115
- Positive 'Love' Body Language: Women 117

Negative 'Love' Body Language: Women _____ 118

Common Body Language Mistakes You MUST Avoid _____ 120

The Body Language Of A Liar _____ 123

Conclusion _____ 131

Do You Like My Book & Approach To Publishing? _____ 132

1: First, I'd Love It If You Leave a Review of This Book on Amazon. _____ 132

2: Check Out My Emotional Mastery Books ___ 132

3: Grab Some Freebies On Your Way Out; Giving Is Receiving, Right? _____ 133

PSS: Let Me Also Help You Save Some Money! _____ 134

Body Language For Beginners

How would you feel if you were asking a junior colleague at work an important question and he or she merely shrugged his or her shoulders without saying a word?

Naturally, you would conclude the person was being knowingly rude.

Albeit being a rude way to say so, in modern society, a shoulder shrug can be an unspoken way to imply *"I don't know"*. A person could utter the words *"I don't know"* and shrug his or her shoulders at the same time, which would appear nicer than the response given by a person who merely shrugs his or her shoulders without saying a word. A shrug devoid of words could appear as if the person is implying *"I don't know or care"*.

Because they occupy sensitive societal positions, politicians, public speakers, and successful public figures often go through body language training to learn the proper use of body language when communicating. One instance of wrong body language from someone such as a politician during a public outing could mean a decline in support.

In college, there were incidences where lecturers would get angry with students who were not concentrating or distracting others. The lecturers would then ask such students to get out of class after calling them out. Then the student would be like, *"But that's unfair, I didn't even say a word"* and the lecturer would reply saying, *"You didn't need to say a word, your attitude said it all"*.

Such a student may not have responded to the lecturer, but the mere fact that their body language was sending out signals the lecturer found disrespectful after the lecturer had called them out meant the student had to leave class.

Control and use of non-verbal communication including body language is a critical must-have skill for all of us because it holds the key to building or destroying relationships.

Another example that shows the importance of body language is that of two waiters, A and B who serve you at restaurants without saying a word to you and while you hand Waiter A a nice tip, you refuse to tip waiter B because you do not like his or her 'attitude'. Unconsciously, it is not that waiter's attitude you dislike, it is his or her body language.

You may be a very hard worker only to discover no one in the office likes you. You then may start wondering why. The answer to this riddle could perhaps be you have a snobbish attitude that displays in how you non-verbally interact and communicate with others.

One thing I remember clearly is that people used to say I look like a very mean and unapproachable person. This often made me wonder why because I am friendly and easy to talk to. However, because that is what my body language said, others did not bother looking behind the mask. Because my body language was negative, they assumed I was a mean person who would probably insult them if they dared say hi.

You do not have bad luck; neither is your lack of designer apparel that makes it hard for others to approach and interact with you. The problem is your body language- you are unintentionally sending out the wrong signals. Although unintentional, your negative body language is off putting to those around you. Not to worry though, in later sections, you shall learn proper body language ethics that will help you attract people and build strong relationships.

Before we get to that, it is only fair we start by cultivating an in-depth understanding of the puzzle that is body language.

What Is Body Language?

Psychologically, body language is the art of communicating without using words. It can be anything you do or any action you take that someone else takes to mean something. Body language is not always intentional; most times, majority of us often fail to realize that others are reading meanings to what we do even when we do not utter a single word.

Each human thinks of him or herself as an amateur psychologist. We all think we can figure people out or read people just by watching them. This is why people conduct interviews; they believe that just by watching you for a few minutes, they can learn a thing or two about you- your personality and possibly, your character.

Human beings are also smart. When you know others are watching and observing you, you continuously work to present yourself in a certain way. You try to control and manage the impressions others have of you.

Managing impressions is the essence of body language- using the right body language to manage the message you send and the impression you leave on others.

Importance of Body Language

Reasons why you should learn effective body language are as many as the lines on your palm. Below are a number of reasons why learning body language is such an important undertaking:

Detecting Insincerity: By properly studying the art of body language communication, you can easily detect when someone is lying or 'cooking' the truth. For instance, when someone avoids eye contact or stammers a lot while communicating, it might mean the person is being insincere. Body language is honest and that is why law enforcement arms of government use it often. Your words may hide the truth, but it is very difficult to hide your body language.

Reinforcement of Words: You can use body language to render more impact to, and reinforce your words. That way, you get people to pay attention to you when you are communicating with them.

Knowing When to Stop: Body language can also help you detect when a person is uncomfortable with a particular conversation or when someone does not like what you are saying. When you know this, you can easily change the topic of conversation.

Expression of Feelings: Another very important use of body language communication is that you can use it to express feelings during communication. A person may say yes when what he or she really means is no. By understanding body language, you detect real intentions without the need for words.

Confidence: You can use body language to show confidence. This is especially important for leaders because followers have to view their leaders as confident and in control. Body language signals such as breaking a sweat, stammering, or being jittery while addressing followers may send out signals that a leader is very unconfident, which may affect the level of trust followers have in such leaders.

Games: If you play games like poker, body language can be a very useful skill to learn because it can give you an idea of your opponent's state of mind and his or her next move.

How Different Parts of Your Body Contribute to Communication

As is determinable, when you use different parts of your body as tools of communication, you send different messages. For instance, while your eyebrows seem irrelevant from a broad perspective, raising one eyebrow (such as what the rock was famous for), could mean puzzlement, or skepticism.

As such, it is only fair we dissect body language and learn the various elements attached to it:

Elements of Body Language Communication

Body language communication has seven major elements. To improve your body language, you must pay attention to these eight areas and improve upon each area.

Facial Body Language

Your face is a very important communication tool. Your face is like a billboard that displays your spoken and unspoken feelings. While the people around you cannot see your physical heart, they can use your facial expressions to read your thoughts, which is why you must pay attention to your facial expressions and what they communicate.

Facial expressions include how you position your eyes, nose, lips, eyebrows and cheeks, or how they move during a conversation. Facial movements help others determine whether you are feeling angry, happy, depressed, or sad.

Facial expressions are usually emotional in nature in that they display emotions. Through facial expressions, it is very easy to detect when a person is happy and when he or she is sad even without talking to the said person.

Facial Body Language

Facial body language further branches into four main categories:

Facial Color

Facial Moisture

Facial Emotions

Facial Expressions

Facial Color

The color of a person's face can say a lot about that person's emotions:

White Face: When a person's face turns white, it means that the person's blood has left the surface and gone deeper to the muscles. This usually happens when a person experiences fear or feels threatened.

Red Face: When a person's face turns red, it means the person's blood has rushed to the surface for cooling down. Strong emotions like anger and embarrassment can cause a person's blood to heat up and rush to the surface for cooling.

Blue Face: When the face or skin has a bluish tinge, it means the person is cold or afraid.

Facial Moisture

The main function of sweat in the body is to act as a cooling mechanism when the body gets hot. Emotional arousal, excitement, or fear can cause a person to get hotter, which would cause more sweat.

Facial Emotions

The following facial signals could also betray your emotions:

Fear: Closed eyes, eyes looking downwards, mouth slightly or wide opened, wide eyes and corners of the mouth turned down could indicate fear.

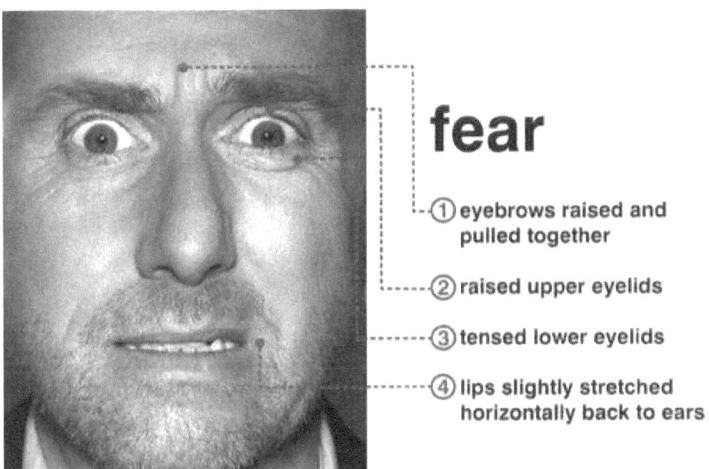

Sadness: Damp eyes, tearful eyes, head down, pinched lips, and eyes cast down indicate sadness.

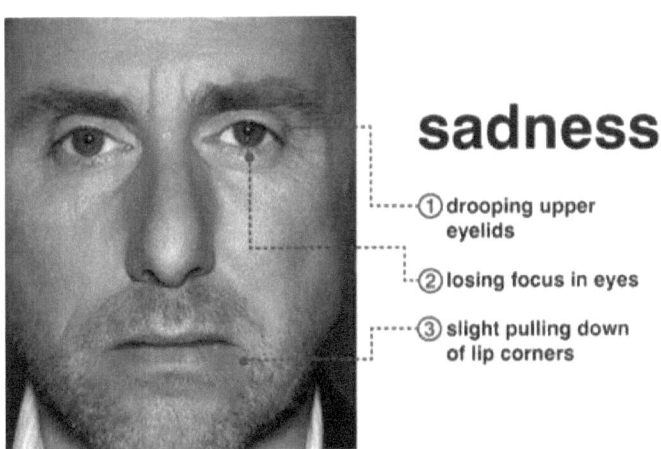

Happiness: Smiling with an open or closed mouth, laughter, sparkling eyes with crows-feet wrinkles on the sides, level head, and eyebrows slightly raised could show happiness.

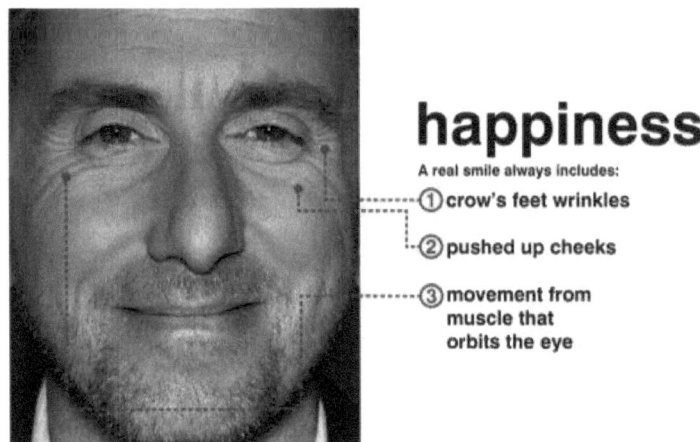

Boredom: Looking away during a conversation, propping up head on hands, turning down the corners of the mouth, and pulling the lips to the side all indicate boredom.

Desire: Dilated pupils with wide eyes, slightly parted lips, smiling, forward head tilt, and slightly raised eyebrows.

Disgust: Flared nostrils, closed mouth with protruding tongue, a head, or eye turn, or twisting the nose in sneer shows disgust.

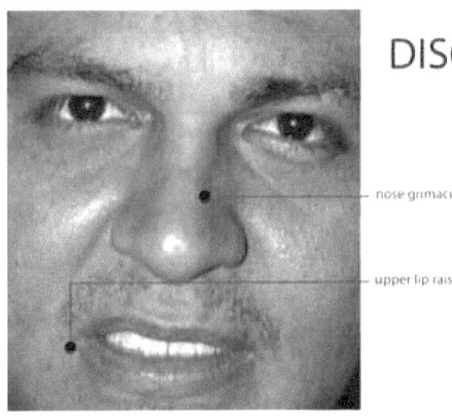

Body Language

DISGUST

Pity: Tilting the head to the side, damp eyes, a slight pulling together of the eyebrows and eyebrows a bit down at the edges all show pity.

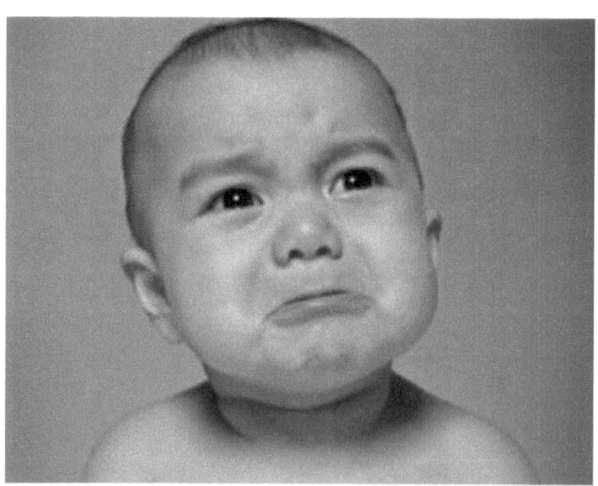

Envy: Staring eyes, closed mouth with corners turned down,

chin jutting, or nose turned down in a sneer all show envy.

Surprise: Eyes wide open, eyebrows raised high, a sideways head tilt or held back, and lowering of the chin indicates surprise.

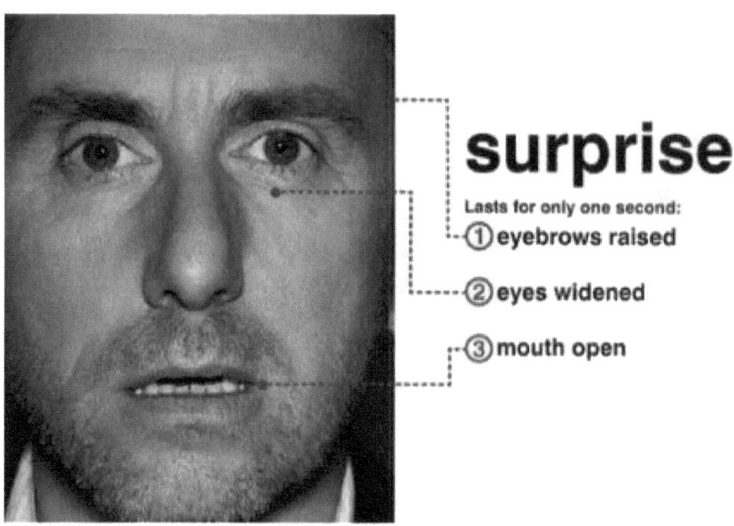

Relief: Smiling, tilting the mouth down on either side, eyebrows lowered on the outer edges.

Shame: Turning the head or eyes down, red flushed skin, or eyebrows held low.

Calm: Mouth turned up at the sides, relaxed facial muscles or a steady gaze.

Body Language

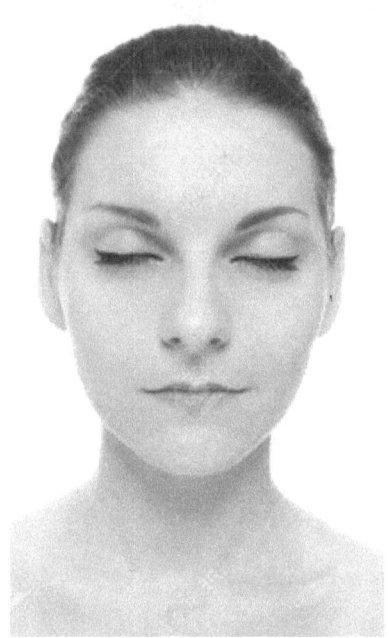

Anxiety: Damp eyes, wrinkled chin, slightly turned down head and a trembling lower lip.

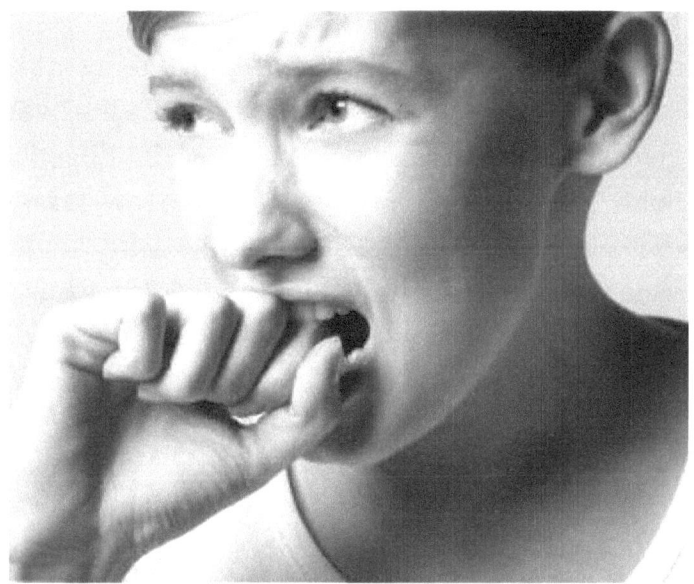

Anger: Clenched and bared teeth, a flattened mouth, jutted chin and a flushed red face, raised eyebrows, corners of the mouth turned down and chin pulled in.

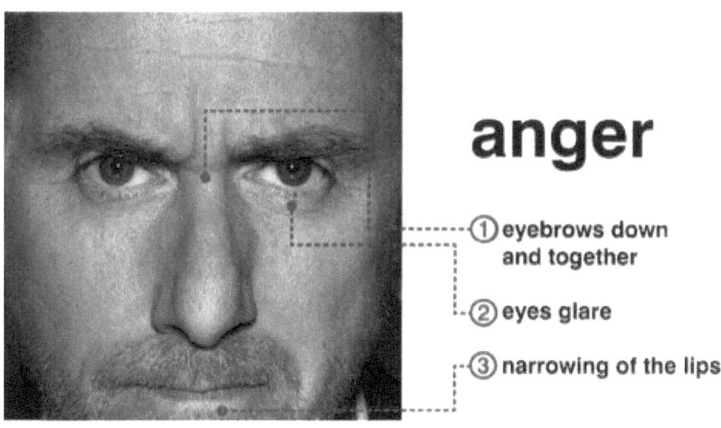

Facial Expressions

Here are some telling facial expressions

Intelligence: There are facial stereotypes for how intelligent a person looks. Society believes people with broad and oval faces with larger chins and smaller noses are less intelligent, while people with larger, prolonged nostrils, narrow faces, and thinner chins are more intelligent. People who smile more are also believed to be intelligent than those whose faces show anger and unhappiness.

Trust: Society also believes a face with a slight smile, slightly raised eyebrows, and the corners of the mouth turned belong on the face of someone confident, friendly, and less anxious, hence worth more trust.

Eye Expression

The eyes are the "window to the soul" for an apparent reason: they send many non-verbal signals that communicate your inner thoughts. You can use eyes to express feelings, emotions, and intentions.

Here are a few eye expressions you should note:

Gazing: When you gaze at something, it means you are very much interested in your focal object. However, a gaze to show interest should be at or above eye level. Looking at a person from head to toe means you are sizing that person up, looking at the lips mean you want kiss them, looking into their eyes indicate love, while looking down over the body indicates lust. A defocused gaze indicates a lack of interest.

Blinking: Blinking is a natural and involuntary process; blinking is the process through which the eye cleans itself. However, an increased blinking rate could indicate stress or insincerity. You could also determine if someone is paying attention to what you are saying when the person blinks when you pause. Rapid blinking indicates arrogance while reduced blinking increases dominance.

Here is an illustration: http://bit.ly/2blinking

Eye Contact: Eye contact is a very important part of conversation. It could indicate affection, dominance, or interest. Here are the various eye contact aspects:

Body Language

Doe Eyes: A major doe eye characteristic is a slight softening and defocusing of the eyes, as well as a relaxation of the eye muscles. This indicates sexual desire.

Eye Contact: When you make eye contact with someone, it signifies acknowledgement and interest. When a person looks away during a conversation, it means you have not grabbed that person's attention.

Break in Eye Contact: Making eye contact during a conversation is good, but prolonged eye contact could be threatening; therefore, look away for some time before resuming eye contact. You could look at the edge of the person's nose because it would still appear as if you are maintaining eye contact. In addition, breaking eye contact suddenly could indicate that a person feels threatened, insulted, or embarrassed. Breaking eye contact suddenly could also indicate flirting.

Prolonged Eye Contact: A prolonged eye contact could indicate a person paying close attention to what you are saying, and could be a sign of romantic attraction.

Limited Eye Contact: Limited eye contact indicates insecurity.

Squinting: An eye squint could indicate sensitivity to light. It could also mean uncertainty, aggression, deception, or flirting.

Looking Down: When you look down during a conversation, it is a sign of submission; however, in some cultures, especially those of Eastern persuasion, it could be a show of respect.

Looking Up: When in a conversation, if the other party looks upwards, it could mean the person is ruminating, bored with what you are saying, or is rendering judgment to what you have said.

Looking Sideways: Looking sideways signifies disinterest. However, moving the eyes from side to side (lateral movements) could be a sign of deception or conspiracy.

Glancing: Glancing at something or someone could mean you are interested in that thing. Glancing at the door during a conversation could signify a readiness to leave. A sideways glance with raised eyebrows indicates attraction, while glancing sideways without raised eyebrows indicates disapproval.

Damp Eyes: Increased dampness in the eyes could indicate tiredness, sadness, anxiety, fear, or recent weeping.

Tearful Eyes: Tears rolling down the cheeks could mean extreme sadness or extreme joy.

Size of the Pupils: When the pupils dilate and become larger, it indicates sexual desire or attraction but when the pupils constrict, it means disgust or that a person is not attracted to you.

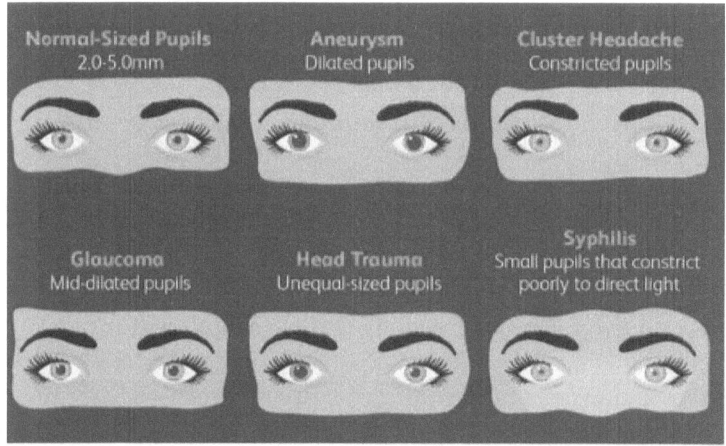

Rubbing the Eyes: A rub on the eyes signifies discomfort; however, rubbing the eyes using a large part of the hand indicates a shy person who is trying to use his or her hand to hide

Staring: Prolonged staring indicates interest, a short stare indicates surprise, while staring back, or locking eyes indicates a challenge.

Following Eyes: Eyes following a particular object signifies interest in that object.

Closing the Eyes: Closing the eyes means avoidance or ignorance; some use this gesture as a way to avoid direct eye contact

Winking: Winking is deliberate and suggests conspiracy or understanding between people.

Gestures

Gestures refer to how you involuntarily or voluntarily move body parts such as your legs, hands, arms, fingers, or your head during conversation. Some common gestures include:

Arms Crossed: Crossing the arms in front of the chest is a sign of defense or disagreement with another person's opinions or actions.

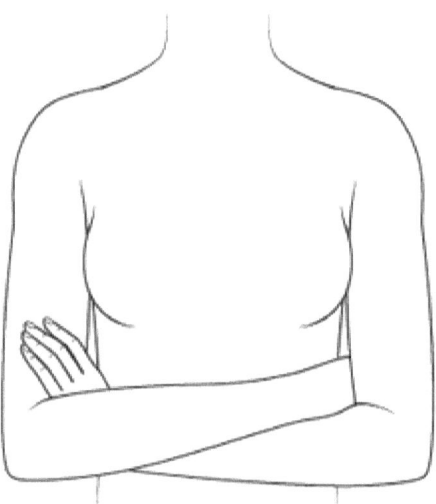

Biting the Nails: Biting your nails during a conversation means you are shy, insecure, stressed, or nervous.

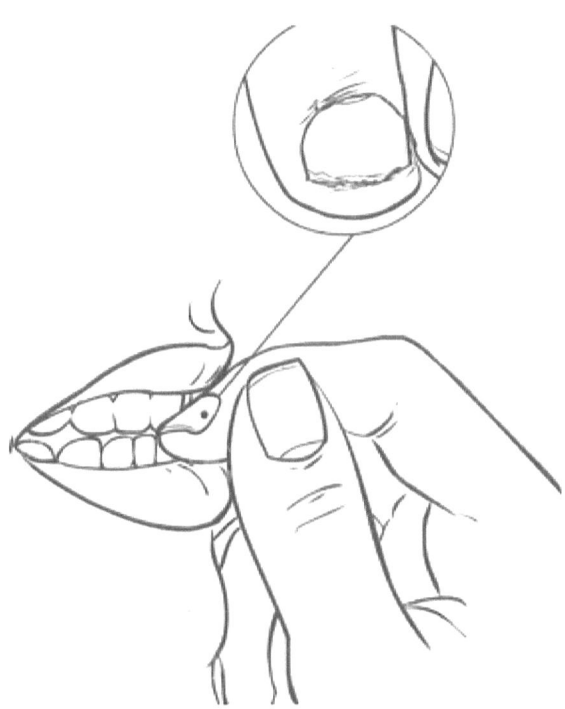

Placing hands on cheeks: This indicates being lost in thoughts or deep concentration.

Having negative thoughts   Female chin stroking   Making decision

Tapping or Drumming with the Fingers: This signifies impatience or tiredness.

Nose Touching or Rubbing: Nose touching or rubbing signifies impatience or tiredness

The nose touch

The eye rub

Briskly Rubbing the Hands: This signifies excitement or eagerness.

Figure 38 *'Isn't it exciting!'*

Steepling: This is when you place your fingers together while pointing upwards; it indicates authority or control.

Body Language

Palms open and facing upwards: This is a sign of sincerity, innocence, or submission.

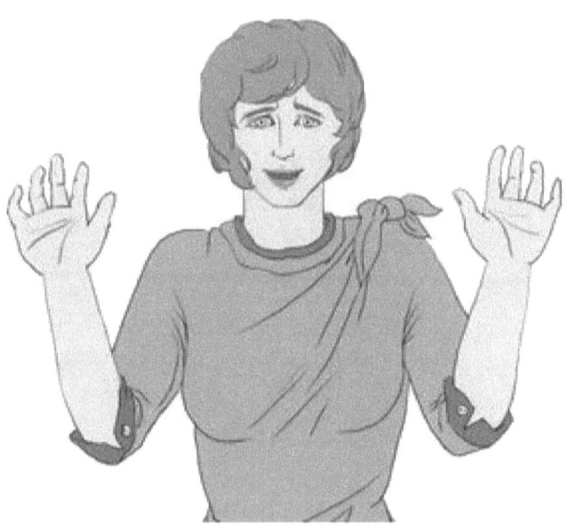

Head in the Hands: This could signify boredom, shame, or being upset.

Ankle Locking: is a sign of nervousness.

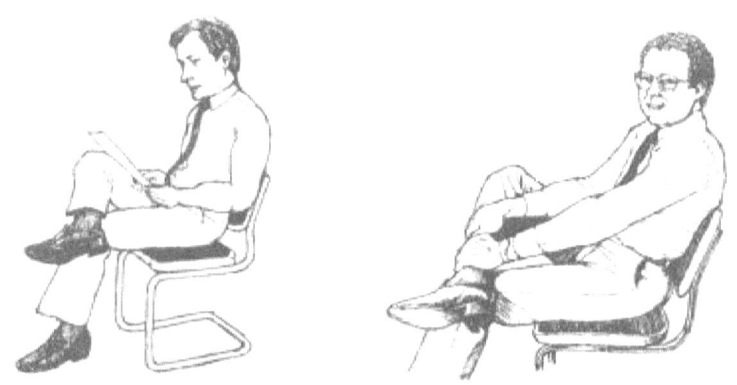

Chin/Beard Stroking: Signifies being in deep thought or trying to come up with a decision.

Pulling the Ears: shows indecision or trying to figure something out

Boredom Gesture

Interested, Evaluation Gesture

Nodding the Head: is a sign of submission or agreement.

Body Language

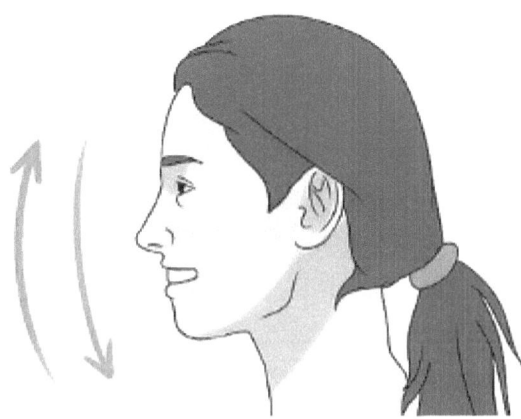

Picking of Imaginary Lint: Picking imaginary lint off your clothes is a sign of disapproval of the other party's opinions or attitude.

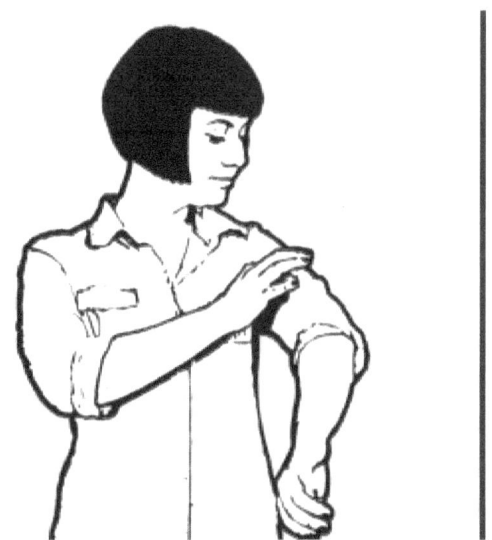

Placing Hands Behind the Head While Sitting: usually shows intimidation or a false sense of security

Body Language

Body Posture

Postures in body language communication are divided into two categories:

1. Open Body Language

2. Closed Body Language

While some people have an open body language while communicating, some people assume a close stance.

Body Language

People who have open body language when communicating are hands-on, interactive, and expressive people. They could also be argumentative or aggressive. Examples of open body language include:

Uncrossing your legs: Uncrossing your legs during conversation while at the same time leaning forward and placing your elbows on your thighs could mean you are worried or are hiding something

Uncrossing the arms: Uncrossing the arms portrays openness and honesty. People who take this stance during communication are frank and honest.

Closed body language on the other hand comes off as having ulterior motives or hidden agendas. If you assume closed body language during conversations, a person good at great reading body language will quickly detect or assume you have hidden motives.

Examples of closed body language during communication include:

Crossing Your Legs while sitting or standing: Crossed legs while sitting imply you are not interested in the other parties' arguments or points. It could imply you intend to argue with the other party. On the other hand, crossed legs while standing imply deep interest in the conversation.

Crossing Your Arms: When you cross your arms during a discussion, it says you have drawn a conclusion or made a decision about the topic of discussion, a decision you intend to defend or protect irrespective of what the other party says. This stance discourages conversation

Placing Your Arms in Front of Your Body: When you place your arms in front of your body during a conversation, you appear nervous or lacking confidence.

Voice

Your tone of voice, pitch, and inflections also matter during conversation. Let us look closely at these:

Pitch: The pitch of your voice can determine your emotions. You could also disguise your feelings during a conversation by changing the pitch of your voice. Excitement makes your vocal cords become tighter, which raises the pitch of your voice. Lowering the pitch of your voice during a conversation shows authority or command.

Inflections and Tone: Inflection refers to the melody and movement of your voice during a conversation. It could indicate interest or loss of interest in the topic discussed. A high-pitched voice and stressing of words for instance indicates deep interest in the topic, while less emphasis on words could mean you are not too interested in what you are saying. To sound nice during a conversation, try matching the pitch of your voice to that of your partner.

Appearance

Coupled with your posture, your dressing and appearance can also send signals during a conversation. The way you dress and appear before others is a part of your communication skills.

The first impression people make about you draws on your visual impact (your dressing and appearance). For instance, carelessly dressing to a meeting could send out the signals of disrespect to the people you are meeting with. Therefore, you should always dress appropriately and appear very neat at all times.

Touch

Touching is another way of communicating; however, touch can mean different things depending on how you do it. A pat on the back for instance, could be a way to encourage someone and at the same time, you can use it to grab someone's attention. One major rule to adopt when touching someone is to touch someone only when you have a bit of personal relation with the person especially if the person is of the opposite gender.

The Art Of Smiling

Smiling plays a great role when it comes to relationships between people, may it be official or unofficial business. Therefore, to improve on your people skills, you need to learn and understand how smiles work. Most people don't understand the power that lies in a smile – you might do everything else right but just because of a smile, you might lose it all.

The earliest studies into smiling were done by a French scientist by the name Guillaume Duchenne de Boulogne, who used electrical stimulation and electro diagnostics to distinguish between a fake smile and real smile. He analyzed how the face muscles worked by pulling them from different angles and recorded the findings.

The Orbicularis oculi – This muscles act independently by causing your eyes to narrow and form the crow's feet i.e. the fine lines and wrinkles around the eye area, which reveals your true feelings.

Zygomatic major muscles – They connect the corners of your mouth and run down the sides of your face. They expose your teeth by pulling your mouth backwards and enlarge your cheekbones; that's why they are used to produce a fake smile because they are controlled consciously.

This can help you distinguish a fake smile from a real smile by just checking the wrinkle lines beside the person's eyes. You can also use this to your advantage since you can be able to fake a smile perfectly without the other person noticing it.

Dr. Wallace V Friesman of the University of Kentucky and Professor Paul Ekman of the University of California designed an easier and effective coding system called the Facial Action Coding System (FACS) to distinguish between a fake smile and a genuine smile. This coding system shows that your unconscious brain causes you to automatically smile when you're happy thus causing a genuine smile.

In depth, what happens is that when you're really happy, you send signals to the part of your brain that processes emotions, which in turn causes your eyes crease up, your eyebrows fall slightly, your cheeks raise and your mouth muscles move upwards to form a smile.

However, there are people who are really good at making fake smiles look almost genuine but the major signs that distinguish an intense fake smile from a genuine smile include the fact that the end of their eyebrows might dip slightly and their eye cover fold moves downwards.

The Magic Of Smiling

Smiling is not only good for you but also for the people around you. So imagine you have the power to make other people happy or just create a positive energy for them by just smiling. This happens when you smile at someone; it forces him or her to reciprocate with a smile as well whether fake or genuine, which creates a good vibrant environment.

Science has been used to prove that the more you smile at others, the better the positive reactions you receive from them. Since smiling is majorly governed by your brain, you'll most likely find yourself mirroring the expressions you see in another person.

This shows that you can use the power of a smile either to change the attitude of a person or to show someone that you are happy and comfortable with them or what they have to offer. In addition, a smile is used as a submission signal to show all is well.

Another factor that most people don't know is that there are different types of smiles that give out different attitudes.

Here are the different types of smiles and what each of them mean.

1) The twisted smile

There are two variations to the twisted smile (you can smile either to the right or to the left) and each will give out a different attitude. The twisted smile to the right of your face happens when the left part of your brain pulls the zygomatic muscles downwards on the right side to form an angry frown.

On the other hand, the twisted smile to your left happens when the left part of your brain raises your left cheek, eyebrow and your left zygomatic muscles to form a cheesy grin. This only means that you can use this smile deliberately to mean one thing, sarcasm.

2) Sideways smile

This is one of the most favorite smiles among men, as it is used to capture the affection of others. That is why it is often used as a courtship gesture even with women.

As a woman, if you use this smile on a man, it makes him want to care for you and protect you. To perform this smile, you look up, turn your head down and away then smile with your mouth closed.

3. The drop-jaw smile

This is where you drop your lower jaw and push both your right and left zygomatic muscles while keeping your upper and lower teeth in contact. This gives an impression of playfulness and laughing to the person seeing the smile. Therefore, it is used to encourage happy reactions from the person receiving the smile.

3) The tight-lipped smile

This smile is mostly used when you want to show that you are not happy about something; you are keeping a secret, opinion or attitude to yourself. This is a classic gesture that most people use especially if they don't like you or they are hiding something from you.

To perform this smile; you need to stretch your lips straight across your face such that your teeth touch each other. Make sure that your lips are as straight as possible.

Body Language

The Power Of Your Hands

How Handshakes And Palms Contribute To Your General Body Language

Did you know that your brain and your hands have more connections than any other parts of your body?

Therefore, it is clear that your hands play a critical role when it comes to communicating with other people and especially your palms. Palms can be used to know when someone is lying, being honest, to show power, submission or dominance. This is how palms contribute to all these things:

How To Use Your Palms To Deceive

Is it possible to lie to someone with your palms visible and they still believe you? The answer is "yes", to someone who does not have a deeper understanding of body language and "no", for someone who does.

Even if you have your palms exposed while telling a lie, other non-verbal cues that are used to detect a lie will be visible. That is why the open palm gesture (which is used to show openness or honesty) will not be effective to pass a lie as the truth if you can't hide all the other lying gestures as well.

How To Use Palms To Detect Honesty/Openness

Palms can also be used to detect if someone is honest or when you want to prove to someone that whatever you are saying is the truth. When you are telling the truth, you are most likely to flash your palms as a way to back up your valid reason or explanation. If you have observed children when they are lying, they mostly hide their palms behind their back. Same case applies to adults especially men who put their arms in the arm-crossed position or in their pockets to hide their palms. This is not so much effective when it comes to women since when they lie, they try to avoid the subject and start engaging in other unrelated activities.

The Palm Command Gestures

Your palms give one of the most powerful body signals that we use to give out directions or commands. The three critical palm command gestures that equip you with the power of silent authority include:

1: The palm-down position

When you issue out instructions or commands with your palm facing downwards, it symbolizes that you are in authority. However, it only works on people who are your subordinates and not your equals or superiors.

This is also evident in couples. If you are keen to observe as couples take a walk or just sitting together, you'll see them holding hands with the man's palm facing downwards holding the woman and the woman's hand facing upwards holding the man. This clearly shows that the man is dominant in the relationship.

The Nazi salute during the Third Reich, had the palm facing down and was used a symbol of tyranny and power.

2: The palm-up position

Your palm facing upwards can mean so many things, like non-threatening gesture, submission or a plea for help or mercy. You cannot pass out commands or instructions with your palm up and you expect it to be authoritative or a must do thing. Therefore, you can use the palm-up position to know whether someone is asking for help, being submissive or meaning no harm.

Body Language

3: The palm-closed-finger-pointed gesture

This is where you clench your fist and use your first finger to give out instructions. This shows you demand total submission and whatever you want to be done is not a request but a must. However, most people don't like to be pointed at since it makes them feel inferior or disrespected. In countries like Malaysia and Philippines, this gesture is not used since it is considered as an insult because it is used to point at animals. That is why they use their thumb to point at anyone or while giving directions.

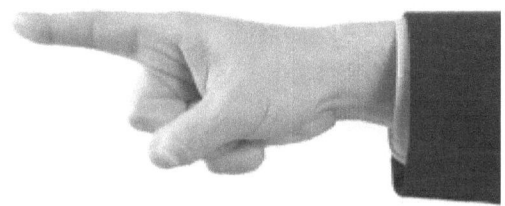

Rules For Accurate Reading Of Body Language

Before diving too much on how you can understand your body language and that of others, it is important for you to know the rules or guidelines to reading someone's gestures. It is not always that what you see or hear that depicts the real attitudes that people may have. That is why you need to learn the three basic and important rules for accurate reading of body language.

Read Gestures In Clusters

More often than not, you'll find that if you use one gesture to determine the attitude of a person, then you will most likely be wrong. It is for a fact that a solitary gesture in isolation of other gestures can mean so many things.

For example, covering a body part can mean so many things – discomfort, habit or even irritation – and this does not necessarily mean that the person is lying to you. Each gesture is like a single word and words can have different meanings but when put in a sentence with other words can bring you to a better understanding of the issue.

Similarly, gestures are grouped together in what we call clusters, which, if utilized appropriately can be used to reveal the truth about a person's feelings or attitudes. Therefore, before you can pass a judgment on a person's gestures, you need to match the person's verbal sentences accurately with their body language clusters. Therefore, as a rule of thumb, always look at gestures in clusters for a more accurate reading and reduce chances of making a mistake.

Read Gestures In Context

Always make sure that when reading gestures, you consider the context in which they occur. If, for example, you see someone sitting alone while facing down and their arms and legs crossed, this would mean that they are just sited thinking of something. However, if the same person used the same gestures while you were trying to sell something to them, then it would mean a lack of interest or rejecting your offer. Therefore, before coming to a decision about a person's body language, always put the context you are in into consideration.

Look for compatibility

Whatever someone tells you verbally should always match with the gestures he or she portrays. Studies show that non-verbal cues carry five times as much impact as verbal cues do and that's why when the two don't match, most people rely on the non-verbal cues and disregard the verbal content.

Someone cannot tell you he/she is happy for you whilst he/she has a frown on his/her face. This clearly shows that the person is most likely lying about being happy for you. Therefore, it is paramount to always make sure that the gestures being portrayed are compatible with what the person is saying. This way, you can get a more accurate and sober understanding of the person's attitude towards the issue at hand.

Observation of gestures in clusters, in the right context and in congruence, is the key to accurately reading the attitude or feelings of a person.

Gender Disparity in Body Language Communication

We have thus far discussed different aspects of body language communication. While we have covered much, you SHOULD note that not all body language is universal. There are gender differences in body language communication because men and women communicate in different ways.

Understanding gender differences in body language communication can help to avoid misunderstandings and miscommunications.

Facial Expressions

There are differences in facial expressions used by men and women. For instance, women smile more than men do because most cultures require that women put a smile on their faces at all times and be more polite.

Proximity

The idea of personal distance and space also differs in relation to gender. Men usually stand far apart from each other regardless of how close or strong the bond between two heterosexual males is. Men also like to create buffer zones between each other using items like cups, coats, or paper. Moreover, men are usually less tolerant of other people invading their personal spaces.

Women on the other hand employ less personal distance

when with other women or even with the opposite gender. However, when in the presence of total strangers especially of the opposite sex, they tend to create or want personal space. However, and this is a generality, a woman's personal space is less likely to be invaded than that of a man.

Male Body Language

Though male body language is not universal, a few body languages are common to most men regardless of culture. Some of them include:

Stance: Men mostly adopt an open body language. They could stand wide apart and spread their legs while sitting or standing to increase their size or show confidence.

Smiling: Most men smile lesser than women do. Men usually adopt a straight or reserved facial expression and only smile when necessary.

Mirroring: is the act of copying the body language of another person whom you are having a conversation with. Although men hardly mirror fellow men, they tend to mirror women to show interest.

Legs and Feet: A man's feet usually points in the direction of his interest. If you are a woman and you want to know if a man is romantically interested in you, you may be able to tell by looking at the direction his feet point.

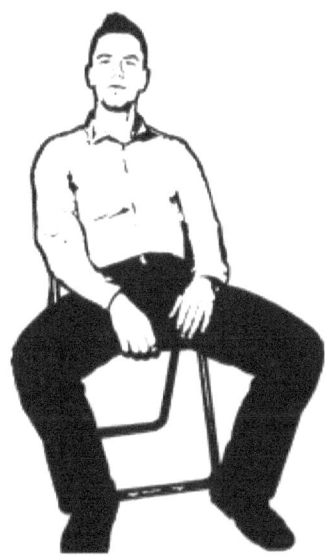

Fidgeting: Men fidget much more than women do. This does not necessarily mean they are insecure; fidgeting in men is just a way to put their energies into use.

Eye Contact: Men make eye contact, but couple it with occasional aversions because eye contact that lasts too long could be a sign of threat or challenge.

Female Body Language

There are some cultural differences in female body language, but some similarities you would find in most females include:

Eye Contact: In women, making eye contact is a sign of interest, while dilated pupils during eye contact signifies a romantic interest.

Smiling: Women smile more than men do; smiling is a woman's way of showing politeness or friendliness.

Body Language

Mirroring. Women mirror other women and men during conversations.

Tapping: Tapping or fidgeting is usually a woman's way of showing discomfort or annoyance.

Touching: Women touch more than men do. Women usually touch each other or touch men too not usually as a romantic gesture, but as a sign of friendliness or as a show of comfort in a person's company.

Body Language

Leaning: In women, leaning forward shows interest, while leaning away could mean displeasure or disinterest.

Body Position: Women usually adopt a closed body language due to upbringing and culture.

The Most Common Female And Male Courtship Gestures And Signals

Common Female Courtship Gestures And Signals

How do you know if a man or a woman really likes you and wants to start a relationship with you? One of the many reasons that you find you are still single after searching and chasing after someone you like is the fact that they have no interest in you or he or she has not portrayed cues to tell you I'm ready and interested in you. Therefore, if you really want to win yourself the woman you like, you need to look out for certain gestures or signals.

In the middle of a woman's menstrual cycle, she becomes more sexually active and acts more provocative towards a man they like. What follows are some of the most common courtship gestures to look out for in a woman to show she could be available.

1. Self-touching

Women have more nerve sensors than men, making them more sensitive to touch sensations. Therefore, if as a man you notice that when you are speaking to a woman she starts sensually stroking her throat, thighs or neck, it infers that if you play your cards right, you might be able to touch her in the same way. Also, self-touching is a way our minds get our bodies to act out our innermost desires thus showing that the woman is imagining what it feels like to be touched by you in the same way.

2. The hair flick and head toss

The head toss and hair flick is usually the most common and first display as a man you will see in a woman that likes you. The woman will flick her head backwards to toss her hair over her shoulder or from her face. Even shorthaired women are no exception; especially the head movements are similar. This is the way a woman shows a man that she can be cute and wants you to view her as one. This gesture allows her to expose her armpits, which gives way for pheromones (sex perfume) to reach her target man.

Body Language

3. Rolling her hips

Women have naturally wider hips than men, which makes it a feature that most men find attractive in a woman. When a woman walks, she has an accentuated roll, which exposes her pelvic region.

This is a powerful sex difference gesture since men cannot walk like that. Therefore, as a man, you need to look out for when a woman rolls her hips – as a subtle courtship gesture that has been used for centuries even in advertising goods and services.

Body Language

4. The knee point

Another courtship gesture to look out for in a woman is when she tucks one leg under the other and points towards the direction you are sited in. This gesture portrays the interest she has in you and what you have to say. In addition, it is a relaxed position and therefore takes out the formalities of a conversation, giving her the opportunity to expose her thighs for you to see.

5. Pouting and wet lips

Pouting is whereby a woman pushes one lip or her bottom lip forward to look sexually attractive. Therefore, most women use pouting and licking of their lips as a way to seduce a man into doing what they want or draw their attention. As a man, if you see any of these gestures in a woman, especially when you interact with her, then it shows she really likes you and you should make your move and court her.

Another gesture to look out for is the slight opening of the mouth. All these gestures simply increase the lip display of a woman, which most men find attractive.

Body Language

6. The shoe fondle

When a woman becomes comfortable in the presence of a man, she becomes relaxed and becomes free with the way she carries herself. One of the ways you can know that a girl is comfortable and interested in you, is when she dangles a shoe on the end of her foot. This is followed by the phallic effect of putting her foot in and out of the shoe.

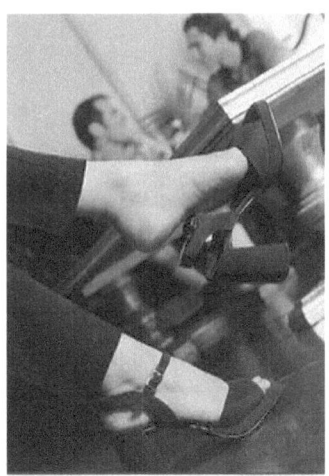

7. Sideways glance

A woman that is interested in you will try and make sure that you notice her. One way a woman can do this is by partially dropping their eyelids then glance at you sideways until you notice her then she quickly looks away. This way, the man will be drawn to her and he'll keep looking at her to find out what she's really up to.

8. Wrist exposure

A woman's wrist area has long been considered as one of the most erotic areas because of the delicate, smooth and soft underside skin. Therefore, as a man, if a woman is interested in you, she will slowly and occasionally expose her wrist to you and increase the rate she flashes it as her interest in you grows. In addition, she will also make her palm visible to you as she speaks.

9. The handbag proximity

A woman's handbag is a personal item that women really

handle with care and don't like anybody, especially men, knowing its contents. So, if a woman likes a man, she will place her handbag in a place that he can see it or even touch it and in other cases, she can ask him to retrieve something from the bag. This is an indication that she is comfortable with the man and she is also interested in forming a connection with him. She can also caress and fondle her handbag as a sign that she really finds you attractive.

10. Leg twine

The most appealing sitting position a woman can assume is the leg twine, which is a gesture that most women use to attract attention. The leg twine is where as a woman, you press one leg against the other firmly to expose the high muscle tone, which shows readiness for sexual performance.

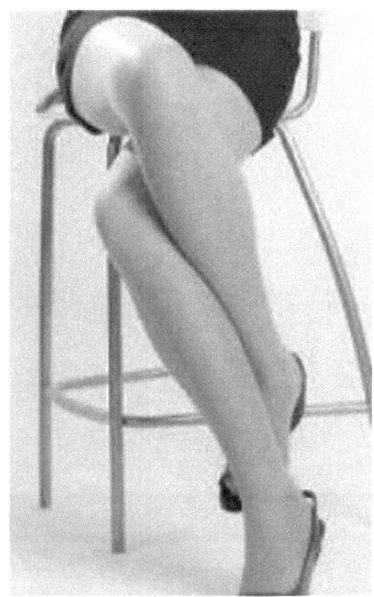

Body Language

Some of the other signals women use includes the crossing and uncrossing of her legs or gently stroking her thighs as a way to show she desires to be touched.

Now let's find out the gestures or signals men display when courting a woman they like.

Common Male Courtship Gestures And Signals

Most men are generally not good when it comes to sending gestures or signals during the courtship period. This is because most male displays involve status, wealth and power. However, this does not mean that there are no male courtship gestures and signals.

Some of the most common male gestures and signals include:

1. Wearing a tie on one side

Men like to feel appreciated and respected (in power) especially with the woman they like. That is why if you're a man and you want to find out which woman likes you, just wear a nice suit but wear your tie slightly off to one side. If the woman you like sees this, she'll be prompted to adjust your tie so that you look good.

2. The thumbs-in-belt gesture

One of the most straightforward gestures a man can use to show he's interested in a woman is the thumbs-in-belt gesture. This gesture allows him to expose his genitals as a sign of dominance. Since most women like men who are dominant, men use this as an opportunity to show a woman he likes her and can be dominant. Some men even kick this up a notch by grabbing their genitals especially while dancing as a sexual display to the woman they want.

3. Preening behavior

Men like it when a woman loves everything about them especially how well groomed they are. That's why, if as a man, you see the woman you like coming your way, your first instinct is to tidy yourself up to look attractive. He may preen by brushing off dust from his shoulder, adjust his tie, rearrange his cufflinks, smooth his collar or his hair.

4. Archer's gaze

We had earlier on discussed how a woman can look into the eyes of a man as a sign she likes him. However, if you are a woman, you can't gaze on a man you like for long because you are most likely to shy off after a while as compared to a man's archer gaze. If as a man you like a certain woman, you'll find yourself gazing at her for a long time and this means you really like her.

5. Muscle flaunting

If as a man you like a woman, you will be prone to show off that you are strong and attractive. Therefore, you will find yourself lifting or handling heavy or technical objects in her presence, wearing tight t-shirts to highlight your muscles or try to flex your muscles in front of her to attract her.

6. One step forward

Another gesture to show as a man you like a certain woman, is where you point your leg towards the direction she is, whether sited or standing. You might then start advancing towards her unconsciously as a way of showing her you'd like to get serious with your relationship with her.

Body Language In Business: How To Use Body Language To Achieve Business Success

Your body language markedly influences your career; it can make or break it. Regardless of your position at your job, or your industry niche, your body language can greatly contribute to your success or failure.

Below are business body language tricks you could adopt to become more successful in business.

Eye Contact and Listening Techniques

When you are in a conversation, the other party is in that conversation because he or she wants to engage in a mutually beneficial conversation (the benefits do not necessarily have to be direct business); therefore, it is good to reciprocate the interest.

The best way to show interest and attentiveness during a conversation is to maintain eye contact. Your eye contact must be subtle and not threatening. You should also avoid interrupting others when they are speaking. Instead, take physical or mental notes as the person speaks, and when it is your turn to speak, voice your points.

Another way to be a good communicator and listener is to nod softly as you listen. This shows you are following the conversation deeply and you are very much interested in the conversation.

Mirroring

Mirroring, or imitating body languages during conversation is another great body language technique that shows you philosophically align with your addressee or addressor. To mirror someone, start by watching his or her sitting position, the way he or she crosses and positions his or her legs, his or her gesticulations, as well as that person's facial expressions. DO NOT do it in annoyingly; be subtle and show cooperation or interest.

Palms Facing Down

When in a business conversation where you want to show authority or leadership, keep your palms facing down. You will notice this subtle but assertive move in most politicians and leaders. It show you are confident and in charge.

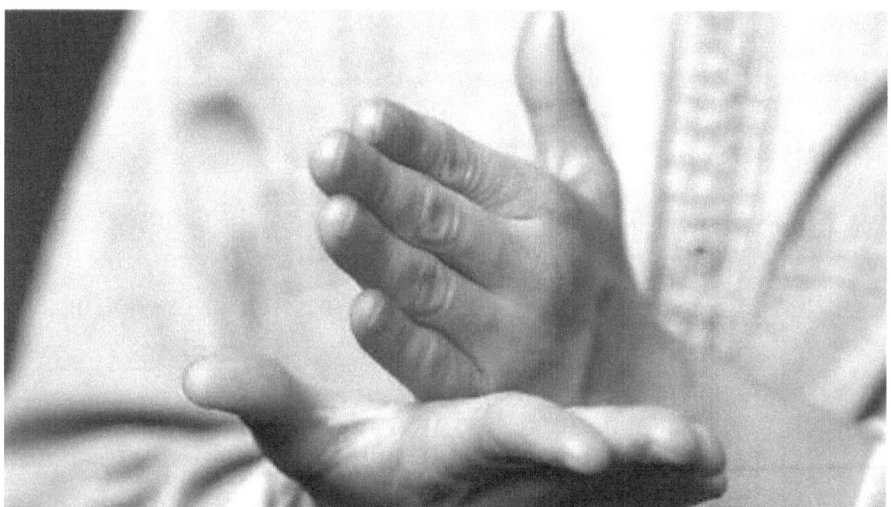

Wide Stance

If you are addressing others, or standing in front of people, you should adopt a wide stance. This stance expands your voice and makes you appear more influential and assertive.

Smiling

Most people can detect a fake or forced smile; hence, when conducting business communication, smile genuinely. A smile makes it easier to talk to you and encourages others to talk to you because of the sense of warmth it projects.

A genuine smile begins slowly, spreads all over the face, and includes the eyes.

Body Movements

You should also reduce body movements because to many bodily movements could be distracting. On the other hand, you should not just stand like a robot, but you should avoid wide gesticulations, fidgeting, squirming, wiggling, and other distracting movements. Your movements should be subtle and used to enhance your communication instead of distracting others.

Handshakes

Nobody likes a limp handshake. However, while handshakes should not be limp, they should not be too hard; they should be firm and natural feeling. A firm handshake communicates trust and respect, while a limp handshake is a sign of weakness or disrespect.

Strong body language communication in business improves your general image and makes you the ideal candidate for leadership positions because good leaders usually have positive body language.

Handshake Styles To Communicate Control And Dominance

Handshakes have been used since ancient times especially when primitive tribes met under friendly situations. They would hold out their arms with their palms exposed to show that they came in peace and concealed no weapon. This has been used over the years and the modern form of this greeting used is the interlocking and shaking of the palms.

What most people don't know is the fact that handshakes transmit attitudes subconsciously. The three main attitudes that are transmitted include submission, dominance and equality, which are key when it comes to relating with other people. Therefore, you need to understand how different handshakes portray different attitudes. In fact, in the 1970, handshake techniques were documented in business skills classes and are still taught as one of the business strategies that can greatly influence a face-to-face meeting.

The submissive handshake

The submissive handshake is where you offer your hand with your palm facing upwards giving the other person control or make them feel in charge of the situation. This handshake is important when it comes to improving relationships with people since you can use it when apologizing or as a sign of respect to others.

However, the palm-up handshake is not always used to show submissiveness since people who use their hands in their profession like artists or surgeons give limp handshakes to protect their hands. That is why, if someone gives you the palm-up handshake, you need to read the gestures that follow in clusters to confirm submissiveness.

If you are a man, you might have noticed that most women give a soft palm-up handshake to highlight their femininity and to show submissiveness.

The dominance handshake

It is evident that most successful management executives use the palm-down handshake to reinforce dominance on their subordinate workers. Therefore, dominance is portrayed by turning your hand to face downwards while shaking the other person's hand.

This tells the other person that you are in control or you want to take control of the encounter. However, you can only use this handshake on people who are subordinate to you and not your superiors or equals. Your palm does not have to directly face down but it has to be on top to communicate you want to gain control. Dominance is quite essential especially in workplaces if you want to gain the respect of your workers or in any situation you want to be in control. This handshake should also be firm to reinforce your authority.

The equality handshake

Not every situation requires you to gain dominance or show submissiveness. In some situations, you just need to give a regular handshake or when you meet someone of equal status as you or a friend, you give them the equality handshake.

The equality handshake is where you shake hands with the other person with your palms in the vertical position. This creates a feeling of mutual respect and equality among the two of you.

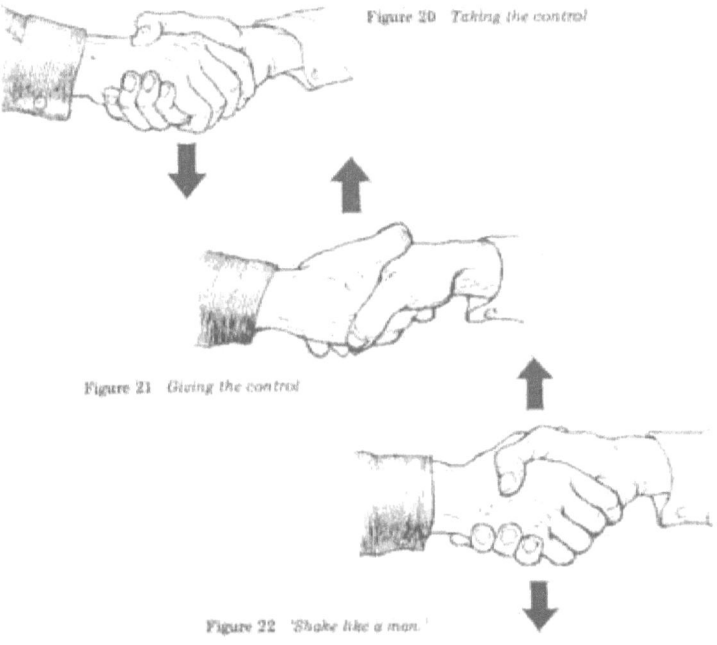

Figure 20 Taking the control

Figure 21 Giving the control

Figure 22 'Shake like a man.'

The right handshake to create rapport

You've seen that handshakes play a great role when it comes to what you are trying to communicate. Creating rapport is one of the most important things when it comes to creating a long lasting relationship or creating a strong bond with someone. Even in a business setup, you need to create a good rapport with the people you meet if you want them to like you.

There are two things to consider when giving out a handshake to create rapport with someone.

- First, make sure that you apply the same pressure on the handshake as the other person by adjusting the firmness to match the other person's firmness.
- Second, make sure that both your palms are in the vertical position so that both of you are equal.

The palm-down thrust

In some cases, you might find yourself in a situation whereby someone decides to take dominance of a handshake by force, leaving you with no other choice but to go into the submissive position. This is what is known as the palm-down thrust, where the person initiates the handshake with their palm facing down then they become aggressive forcing you into the submissive position. If you happen to find yourself in such a situation, the best way is to gain back control of the handshake with other techniques.

Some of these counter techniques include:

1. **The hand on top technique**

One of the techniques to disarm a power player is by using your other hand to change the position of the handshake.

You just shake his/her hand with your palm facing upwards then place your other hand on the top part of his hand (the one on the handshake) into the double-hander and slowly straighten the handshake. This will effectively switch the power from them to you and it is quite easy and effective to use.

However, you might come across a power player that makes it difficult to apply the above technique, especially if he/she does it purposefully and regularly to intimidate you. What you do is that the next time he/she tries to shake your hand, grab on top of his hand or wrist then shake it. This method should only be used as a last resort after trying the double-hander technique severally.

2. **The step-to-the-right technique**

The hand on top technique might not work in some cases since not only is it obvious when you do it but also hard. When it comes to the step to the right technique, you have the ability to switch the handshake position without the other person even realizing it.

You begin by stepping forward with your left foot as you reach to shake the other person's hand. Next, bring your right leg forward into the person's space then bring your left leg again to your right leg to complete the cycle.

Lean in and shake the person's hand. You will be able to straighten the handshake easily since you'll have invaded the person's personal space. Just train yourself to step into a

Body Language

handshake with your left foot so that it can be easier for you to disarm a power player.

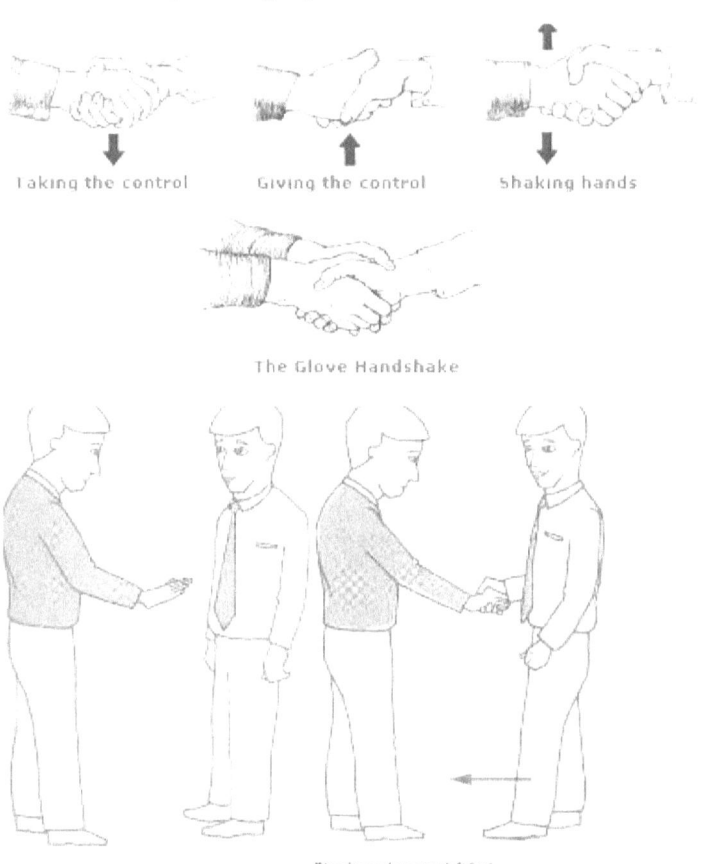

Body Language

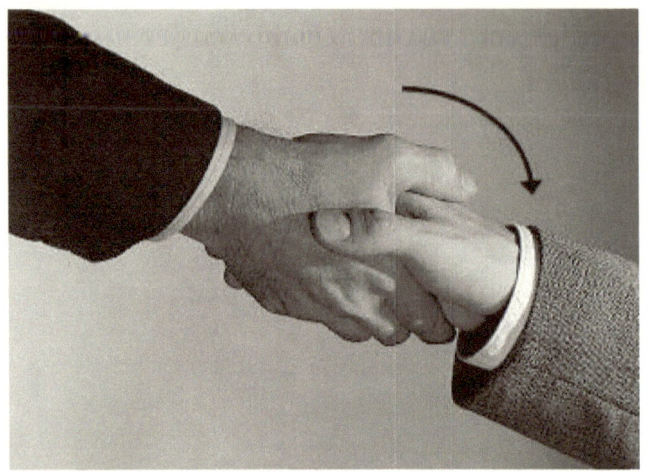

The Intimacy And Control Handshakes

A two-handed handshake is meant to show trust, sincerity or depth of feeling for the person receiving the handshake.

There are four common control handshakes, which include the shoulder hold, the wrist hold, the upper-arm grip and the elbow grasp. The only difference between the two-handed handshake and a normal handshake is that you introduce your left hand into the handshake to convey more intimacy and control.

If you're the one to initiate the handshake, you are only allowed to do the elbow grasp and the wrist hold only where one person feels close to the other since your left hand enters into the personal space of that person. The upper-arm grip and the shoulder hold are used to show close intimacy and may even result into a hug.

In addition, it gives you the opportunity to use your left hand to communicate the depth of your feelings and control the receiver's movements

Keep in mind that you can only use these two-handed handshakes on people you have a bond or close to and not just anyone. In addition, if anyone gives you a two-handed handshake and you're not close then you need to find out what they are up to.

Body Language

The upper arm grip

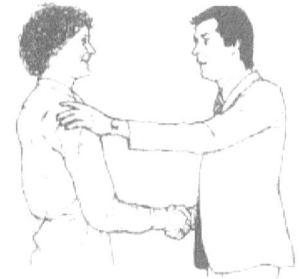
The shoulder hold

Do you know that you can practice all these handshakes but still fail at creating a good relationship with others? The problem is that you are not doing the handshake properly and maybe you don't even realize it. That is why you need to learn about the worst handshakes that you should avoid.

They include:

a) The pump stroke handshake

This is where you take the other person's hand vigorously and you rhythmically stroke it up and down non-stop such that you make the other person uncomfortable.

You will even notice that he or she will try to pull away from the handshake. You need to understand that the average normal handshake takes about six pump strokes and anything more than this is not a good gesture and the person receiving the handshake will not be happy about it.

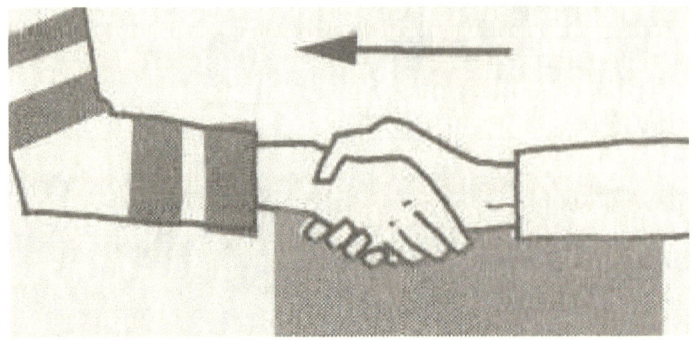

b) The Dutch handshake

This handshake originates from the Netherlands where you give a person a handshake but you don't enclose your palms together. You hold the person's fingers tightly across the fingers such that they remain horizontal.

As you can see, this handshake is less clammy to the touch and that's why it is a wrong way to give anyone such a handshake.

c) The arm pull handshake

This is an aggressive form of handshake where the person giving the handshake pulls the other person's arms. Consequently, if you are the one giving the handshake, you might end up hurting the other person's arm, which is not good.

It is normally used when you want to keep people away from your personal space. You might not even notice as you do it but it's wrong and nobody likes it. Just try to be gentle and avoid pulling the other person's arm too much while shaking their hand.

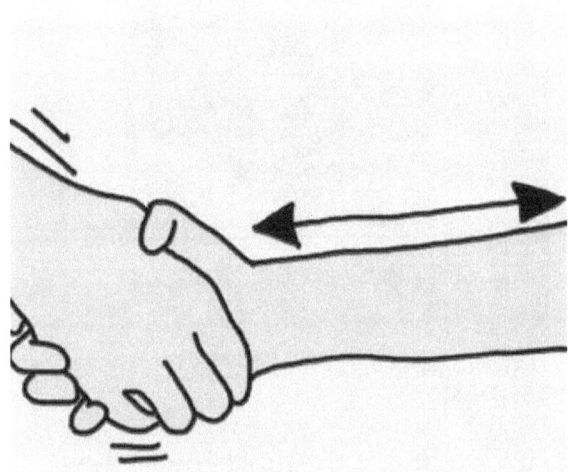

d) The hand-crusher handshake

This is one of the most common and most hated handshakes of them all. Not only does it hurt the other person's hand, it also shows lack of respect for that person.

If you are the one shaking a person's hand, you'll hold their hand in a tight grip such that you compress their knuckles tightly together until they are in pain. This is so especially if you are stronger than they are or when you're trying to give a firm handshake but end up over doing it. Therefore, you need to avoid this type handshake at all cost and try as much as possible to give a firm yet gentle handshake.

e) The wet fish handshake

The wet fish handshake is also one of the most common yet uninviting greetings. This handshake happens when you shake someone's hand with a soft, clammy or cold palm.

It only shows that you have a weak character and that you are afraid or anxious of what is about to happen. Therefore, it sends a very bad message to the receiver who will feel your lack of commitment to the meeting.

In most cases, you'll even find that your palm is sweaty and even shaking which can be noticed when someone shakes your hand. This is because your palms have more sweat glands than any other part of your body and so sweating your hands is easy. That's why you need to carry a handkerchief just in case you need to wipe your palms before a handshake.

Cultural Gesture Differences

Do you know that different cultures have different gestures on similar situations? Most of the gestures may be same but may vary with the culture. Therefore, you need to be aware of this cultural gesture differences since at a certain point, you are bound to come across a person with a different culture from yours.

For example, the Western and Eastern cultures dictate that one blows his/her nose into a handkerchief while the Japanese and Asians snort or spit on the ground. This habit has left the Westerners and Europeans repulsive to this habit of spitting by the Asians and Japanese who term it as a healthier option. Another cultural gesture that differs with these two cultures is a man wearing a handkerchief on the top pocket of his jacket. The Asians do not like this habit since they argue that the person will use that handkerchief and still put it back into their pocket, which is unhygienic.

Another common gesture that varies with different cultures is being touched while having a conversation. There are those people who touch others, as they speak and don't mind being touched as well while the other person speaks but there are those who find it offensive.

For example, the French culture allows people to touch each other as they speak while the British culture does not support touching each other as you speak unless its sports related.

The Most Common Cross-Cultural Gestures

1. The V-sign

The V-sign has been used since the Second World War where Winston Churchill popularized it as the 'V for victory'. His version entailed flushing out the first and second finger to form a 'V' with your palm facing out.

However, the modern form of this sign is done with your palm facing you to show someone to "chill out" or relax and it is a greeting from a far.

2. The zero sign

This gesture involves you using your thumb and first finger to form an "o" then you stretch the other remaining fingers as shown in the image below.

This gesture is used to symbolize "OK", which stands for 'everything is fine' while others believe it stands for 'KO' that means 'knock-out'.

There is yet another theory that explains this gesture originated from the place of birth of the nineteenth century president of America, which was Old Kinderhook.

The theory explains that this was the president's campaign slogan at that time and that is why some people believe this is the real meaning of the gesture.

However, people from different parts of the world have a different meaning for this gesture and that's why you need to investigate what it means before using it in your area. In Belgium and France it is used to mean 'nothing' or 'worthless' while in Japan it is used to mean 'money'. In Arabian countries it is used to mean obscenity or as a threat signal.

Body Language

3. The thumbs-up gesture

This gesture is commonly used in Britain, New Zealand and Australia and is used to mean 'up yours'. In countries where the British influence is strong such as the United States of America, New Zealand and South Africa, this gesture can be used to mean two things.

- When you use this gesture with your thumb sharply upwards, it becomes an insult to the other person.

- It is used as an OK signal to show you're okay or when asking the other person if everything is fine.

The Language Of Hands

Your hands play a critical role when it comes to your body language. Most of the time you won't even notice that you're using your hands in your conversations and they send a message to the people around you. Therefore, you need to understand what message you pass across when you use your hands as you speak or as you listen.

Putting your hands behind your back

The message you send when you walk or stand with your hands behind your back is that you are superior to the rest, you're in power or you're confident. That is why the British Royal family and other powerful people mostly use this gesture. The gesture puts forward your most vital organs – your chest, stomach and your heart – and that is why it is used to show fearlessness or power.

There are several variations to putting your hands behind your back and they include:

1. **The palm and hand grip**

This gesture involves you putting both your arms behind your back then interlocking your palms together. It is one of the most common gestures when it comes to putting hands behind your back and it is used when you want to feel confident or to show authority.

2. The wrist grip gesture

The wrist grip gesture is used to show frustration or self-restraint when you are trying to prevent yourself from striking out or when you're impatient. You can perform this gesture by placing both your arms behind your back, and then you use one of your palms to grasp the wrist of the other hand.

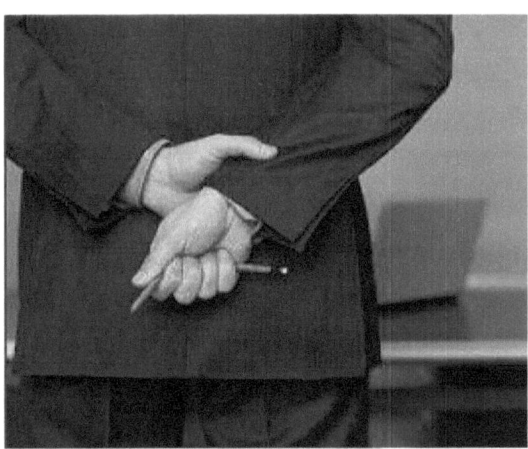

Aside from putting your hands behind your back, there are hand gesture that you use with your hands in front of you.

Some of these gestures you might have noticed them but maybe you didn't know what they mean.

Here are some of the hand gestures you do with your hands in front of you.

1. The steeple

This gesture involves you pressing the fingers of one hand slightly to the fingers of your other hand. The gesture is normally used to show a confident attitude or superiority and it doesn't have to be that your fingers are the only ones touching each other; you can also put your palms together to form 'the praying hands'. However, when you change into the praying hands, you pass a different message that you are God-like or that you are begging for mercy from a superior person.

There are two main variations to the steeple gesture and they include; the raised steeple, which is used when you are giving out what you think and the lowered steeple, which is used when you are listening to someone speak.

The steeple gesture is mostly used to give out a positive message and can sometimes be misinterpret as a negative one. That's why you need to put the context of the gesture into mind and interpret the gesture in clusters so as to give a more accurate interpretation.

2. The clenched hands gesture

At a quick glance, you might think that the clenched hands gesture indicates courage or fearlessness but it's not. If you take a closer look at the gesture and when it is mostly used, you'll discover that it is mostly used when you're anxious or holding back something that is not good.

This is especially the case when you are conducting negotiations or when being questioned. The clenched hands can be positioned either in front of your face or on your lap when you're sited or in front of your pelvic region while standing and the level of your frustration can be measured with which position you place your clenched hands. Placing them in front of your face shows that you are more frustrated than when you place your hands before your pelvic area.

Hands clenched in raised position

Hands clenched in middle position

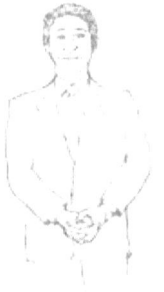
Hands clenched in lower position

3. Rubbing of palms

In most cases, you'll find yourself rubbing your palms together when you are anticipating a good thing or when you are about to unveil something to the benefit of the person you're speaking to.

However, you need to rub your palms quickly if you want to pass this message since if you do this slowly, it will be termed as devious or sneaky. In addition, you also need to read this gesture in context because people rub their hands when they're cold.

4. The thumb and finger rub

Rubbing your thumb and your first finger together shows that you are expecting money from the other person. Its symbolism is the rubbing of a coin between your index finger and your thumb. You should avoid this gesture because it carries with it a negative connection with money such as bribery.

Body Language And Love: How To Use Body Language To Nurture Personal Relationships

When you are in love, there are instances where you wish you could read your partners mind to know what he or she is thinking or feeling. While it is impossible to read your partner's thoughts and mind, you can read your partner's body language and use it to determine what he or she is thinking or what he or she is feeling at a particular point in time.

However, there exist gender body language differences when it comes to how men and women differences show love, romance, and affection. A man's body language usually differs from that of a woman.

Positive 'Love' Body Language: Men

Holding Hands: If a man holds your hands often especially in front of friends and family, it means he is really 'into you' and does not even notice that he is holding your hands. This is especially true if he is the one reaching for your hands more often. It means he is proud of you, not afraid to show you off, and sees both of you more as one person than as a separate entity.

Body Language

Hair Touching: A man would generally treat you well and complement your beauty but when he's nursing the idea of getting serious with you, he begins to notice a few intricate details about you like your freckles, your scars, birthmarks, and other imperfections in a bid to get to know you better. When a man touches your hair however, it is a sign that he cares about you especially if he does it in public.

Sitting on the Floor: When a man sits on the floor around you, it means he is comfortable around you, feels less intimidated, and would like to have deep, meaningful conversations with you.

Wrapping Arms around You in Public: Wrapping your arms around a woman is a man's way of saying "Back off, this one is mine." A man not sure, if he wants a woman in his life long term usually keeps a distance from her especially in public. When he makes bold moves like wrapping his arms around you in public, it simply means he is trying to publicly 'claim ownership' of you.

Negative 'Love' Body Language: Men

Men also have negative romance body language signs that could mean that he is not really into you. These negative signs include:

Avoiding Eye Contact: A man who constantly avoids a woman's eyes during conversation may be a cheat or a deceiver

Excessive Touching: If a man touches a woman a whole lot, or looks down a lot when in the presence of the woman, that man might be insecure about the relationship.

Big Body Movements: A man who makes big body movements or constantly tries to invade a woman's personal space uninvited might be a controlling man.

Walking Ahead: A man who walks ahead and not beside a woman so that she has to work to keep up with him might be a selfish man

Starring: If a man stares at you too much, or makes intense eye contact, he is the jealous type.

Positive 'Love' Body Language: Women

When it comes to love, women often display the following positive body language:

Rolling the Eyes: In women, a roll of the eyes is a sign of disinterest or disgust

Intense Look: If a woman likes a man, it is usually evident in how she looks at him. If she looks at him very intensely, it shows she likes him especially if she raises her eyebrows, holds eye contact, or blinks rapidly.

Body Language

Hair Touching: When a woman is playing with her hair during a conversation, it may mean that she is bored with the conversation or that she wants the man to kick things up a notch.

Arching her Back: When a woman aches her back such that her legs and breasts become more evident, this is a sign of attraction

Giggling: A woman who giggles a lot while holding a conversation with a man wants the man to know that she is really interested in the conversation and probably likes the man a lot.

Negative 'Love' Body Language: Women

Negative love body language in women includes:

Freezing Up: If a woman abruptly stops making a gesture or suddenly stops talking, it could signify discomfort, insecurity, or anxiety

Placing Barriers: If she use her friends, people around, or objects to create barriers, that is a sign she is uncomfortable

A Blank Stare: If she has a blank stare on her face, she is not interested.

Frowning: While frowning can sometimes show disinterest, it can also mean feigned disinterest especially if a woman is playing hard to get.

Common Body Language Mistakes You MUST Avoid

We have spent the last few sections learning a few body language tricks that will improve your communication skills in general and help you become more successful. This section will outline a few body language mistakes you SHOULD avoid if you want to appear emotionally intelligent and a good communicator.

Avoid Slouching: Slouching is something you should never do because slouching often appears as a sign of disrespect or a sign of disinterest. Standing tall and maintaining an upright position, however, signifies power and authority. It is also a way to signify strength.

Exaggerated Gestures: People can read exaggerated and false gestures just as well as they can read genuine ones. Therefore, AVOID false or exaggerated gestures when making conversations especially when addressing a crowd.

Looking at the Clock: Constantly glancing at your watch shows you are bored, with the conversation; the other party might get the wrong signal and hurriedly finish the conversation if he or she notices your constant staring at the clock when he or she is talking to you.

Turning Away From People: Do not turn away from people when you are talking to them. Turning away says you are not comfortable around them or that you do not trust them. It could also mean you are disinterested in talking to them.

Folding Your Arms: We mentioned in an earlier chapter that folding your hands when talking to someone means you have made up your mind about the topic in discussion and no matter what the other person says, you are not going to change your mind; this makes others feel uncomfortable talking to you

Inconsistency: Your facial expression must align with your words. If your facial expression looks angry and your words seem soft, people will feel uneasy around you and may even distrust you.

Fidgeting: Constant fidgeting during conversation makes you look self-obsessed. If you are in a business conversation, it just might make you look unserious with your career and much more concerned with your physical appearance.

Rolling your Eyes: Rolling your eyes is a sign of disinterest or disrespect; avoid rolling your eyes especially in business conversations.

Clenched Fists: Avoid clenched fists because they show anger, being argumentative, or being defensive.

Personal Space: Respect other people's personal spaces especially if you do not have a personal relationship with them. Invading someone's space makes him or her feel uncomfortable around you.

Texting: When in a conversation, put your phone away.

Texting or playing with your phone shows disinterest in what the person is saying or that the person on the other end is much more important.

Rubbing your Hands Together: Rubbing your hands together during a conversation is a sign of nervousness or discomfort

Your dressing is also a very important part of your body language. If you dress badly, even if you master all these tips, you may end up sending out the wrong signals. Hence, while improving your body language, improve your dressing too so that everything aligns.

Ever found yourself in a situation that your hands are tied just because of ignoring the small minor things that matter? How many times has your partner told you that they are fine when in reality they are not ok? Would you like to be able to detect when someone tells you "I'm fine" but deep down they're screaming for help? This is how to detect the body language of a liar.

The Body Language Of A Liar

Part of fostering healthy and strong relationships is by being able to detect when the other person is lying to you. This way you'll be able to become familiar with how the other person acts and establish a baseline.

Basically, this baseline is how the person (that you are concerned about) acts under normal conditions or when telling the truth. Sadly, you can't be totally sure when someone is not being honest with you because some people have mastered the art of hiding the truth so well.

However, if you are keen enough with the things we are about to discuss, then you are more likely to detect when someone is lying to you and continue strengthening your relationships with them.

Here are some of the signs you can use to tell that someone could be lying:

1. **Shifty eye movements**

During a conversation with someone, especially if it's a serious topic, pay attention to how they move their eyes. A person who has nothing to hide will look you straight in the eyes as you talk with minimal shifting of the eyes.

In addition, if you are talking to someone you are used to, you will notice that they tend to look at a certain direction when thinking of something. Therefore, chances are high that when you ask them a question and they look to the opposite direction (to where they normally look when thinking) then they are lying to you. This is not a definite assurance that they are lying but it is an excellent tool to use to tell when trying to know if someone is lying to you.

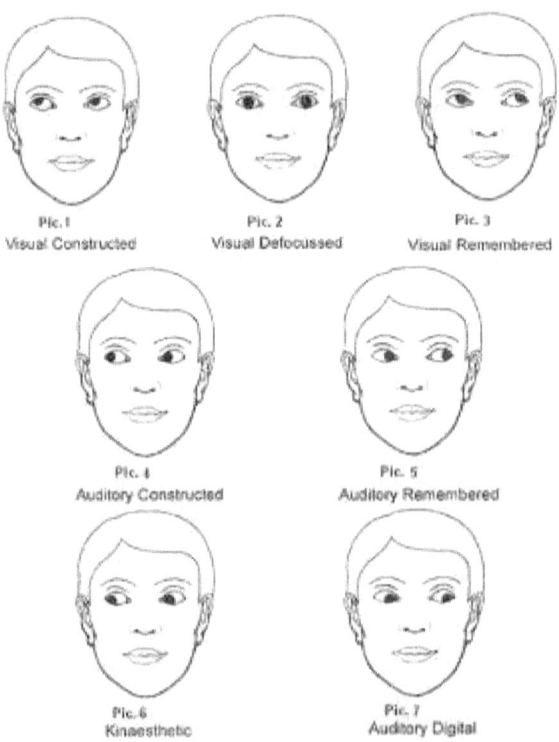

2. Balance in stability

Another way you can tell if someone is lying to you is by looking at their stability as they talk to you. When someone is lying, they tend not to remain steady as they talk to you and instead they keep moving from one spot to another.

Body Language

In other instances, you will see the person putting more weight on one foot such that they become asymmetrical so they keep shifting from one foot to the other more than usual. This asymmetry is brought about by the dissonance between the left and right hemisphere of the brain; therefore, it is like the body's way of saying "something is wrong".

3. Tilting their head

Asymmetry is not just tied to the lower region of the body but also to the inclination of the other person's head. A cocked head is an indication of asymmetry since it shows the lack of certainty and chances are high that the person is not being completely honest with you. Again, it is not a complete assurance that they are lying so be on the lookout for the other signs so as to be more sure.

4. Smirking instead of smiling

When a person is talking to you, it is wise to pay attention to their face. When a person smirks instead of smiling, he or she may be sending a message that what they are saying is not completely true (that is the body's way of showing discontent with the information).

This could be anything from a fake smile to a full on smirk.

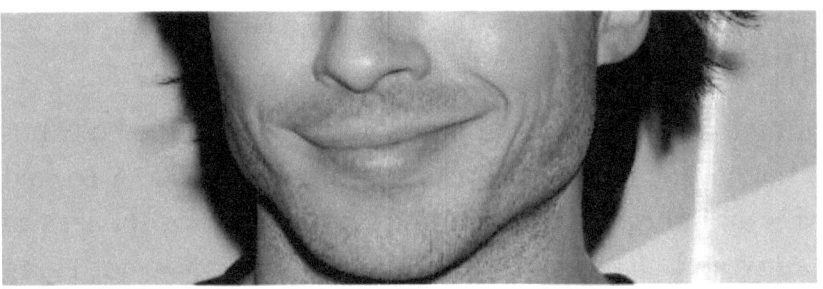

5. Detachment from their normal body language

If you've taken time to know a person, you can predict all their body language under different situations. Therefore, if you want to be able to strengthen a bond with anyone, you need to get acquainted with their normal mannerisms.

A significant departure from these normal mannerisms especially when you engage with them can be an indication that the person is lying or hiding the truth from you.

There might be some few reasons why the person might be behaving differently than their normal self and not necessarily because they are lying. That is why this skill requires a keen eye because in most cases, if someone differs from their normal mannerisms especially if you interact with them, they are most likely to be lying or hiding the truth from you.

6. A blinking rate that is more than normal

When you are mentally stimulated, your blink rate may go down due to the cognitive overload or it may go up as you attempt to come up with a false story or as you become increasingly anxious. Therefore, if you see that the person you are talking to has an increased blink rate than normal, then the person is most likely lying to you.

7. Pointing more than usual

When someone lies to you and they are afraid you might find out, they result to defensive mechanisms to protect themselves and turn tables on you. That is why when you confront the person about a lie they've told you, he or she may decide to take up aggressive gestures like pointing so as to deviate the attention from them.

8. Difficult for them to speak

A telltale sign of someone who is lying to you is that the person will find it hard to speak especially if you are on to them. If you've seen someone being interrogated, then you've noticed that he or she will be confident and sure about what they are saying at first but as the questions become more and more difficult, they begin to stammer and even keep quiet.

Therefore, if you are talking to someone about something and you notice that they are having difficulties telling you the story, then they are most likely to be lying. This occurs since the automatic nervous system of our bodies decreases salivary flow during times of stress, which in turn dries out the mucus membrane of the mouth making it difficult to speak.

9. Instinctively covering parts of the body

If you see someone instinctively covering vulnerable body parts like their head, chest, throat or abdomen as they talk to you then they are most likely lying to you. This is especially if they don't normally do this when they talk. This is like the body's way of saying whatever you are saying or being told "has hit" the wrong nerve.

In addition, another most common thing people do when they are telling a lie is that they will automatically put their hands over their mouth since they don't want to answer or deal with the issue at hand. This simply indicates that the person doesn't want to reveal everything and they're not being completely honest with you.

10. Giving out too much information

When someone is telling a lie, they tend to go on and on giving too much information about a topic. Therefore, if you confront someone about a topic and you notice that they are giving out excess information that you've not requested or an excess of detail then he or she is most likely lying to you. This occurs since the person lying to you wants to give you much information hoping that with their openness and talking, you'll believe them.

Creating a connection with someone is not easy and that is why you need to be able to create a bond with someone in good times and bad times.

Therefore, if you find that you can tell when someone is not being completely honest with you then you can say you have a healthy and strong relationship with him or her.

Conclusion

We have come to the end of the book. Congratulations for reading until the end. It shows you have real commitment to transform your life positively.

Improving your body language is something you have to devote time and effort to just as you would if you were learning a new language.

The next step is to use the information you have learned from this book to improve your body language.

Do You Like My Book & Approach To Publishing?

If you like my writing and style and would love the ease of learning literally everything you can get your hands on from Fantonpublishers.com, I'd really need you to do me either of the following favors.

1: First, I'd Love It If You Leave a Review of This Book on Amazon.

2: Check Out My Emotional Mastery Books

Note: This list may not represent all my Keto diet books. You can check the full list by visiting my author page.

Emotional Intelligence: The Mindfulness Guide To Mastering Your Emotions, Getting Ahead And Improving Your Life

Stress: The Psychology of Managing Pressure: Practical Strategies to turn Pressure into Positive Energy (5 Key Stress Techniques for Stress, Anxiety, and Depression Relief)

Failure Is Not The END: It Is An Emotional Gym: Complete Workout Plan On How To Build Your Emotional Muscle And Burning Down Anxiety To Become Emotionally Stronger, More Confident and Less Reactive

Subconscious Mind: Tame, Reprogram & Control Your Subconscious Mind To Transform Your Life

[Body Language: Master Body Language: A Practical Guide to Understanding Nonverbal Communication and Improving Your Relationships](#)

[Shame and Guilt: Overcoming Shame and Guilt: Step By Step Guide On How to Overcome Shame and Guilt for Good](#)

[Anger Management: A Simple Guide on How to Deal with Anger](#)

Get updates when we publish any book that will help you master your emotions:
http://bit.ly/2fantonpubpersonaldevl

To get a list of all my other books, please fantonwriters.com, my author central or let me send you the list by requesting them below: http://bit.ly/2fantonpubnewbooks

3: Grab Some Freebies On Your Way Out; Giving Is Receiving, Right?

I gave you a complimentary book at the start of the book. If you are still interested, grab it here.

[5 Pillar Life Transformation Checklist](#): http://bit.ly/2fantonfreebie

PSS: Let Me Also Help You Save Some Money!

If you are a heavy reader, have you considered subscribing to Kindle Unlimited? You can read this and millions of other books for just $9.99 a month)! You can check it out by searching for Kindle Unlimited on Amazon!

www.ingramcontent.com/pod-product-compliance
Lightning Source LLC
Chambersburg PA
CBHW030154100526
44592CB00009B/273